THE MAGIC READER

BY LOUISE GUHL

W0006806

BOOK 1

To Dr. Guy Duckworth, Professor Emeritus of Music at the University of Colorado, Boulder, I give thanks for what he taught me about the learning process.

I wish to thank my friends and colleagues, Gwendolyn Cline Perun and LeRene Soderberg, who tested this material on a large number of students.

Contents

ISBN 0-8497-9380-7

Preface to Teachers

The emphasis of **The Magic Readers** is on the reading process and the ability to keep the beat. **The Magic Reader** series has produced amazing results by the many students (of several teachers) who have used it. The series has also been successful when used with insecure readers who have already been studying one or two years. Although written originally for beginners age seven and up, this method has also given adults a quick and sturdy beginning with playing the piano.

The Magic Reader, Book 1 is preparation for the primer level of any method. By starting with **The Magic Reader, Book 1**, the student develops a strong sense and knowledge of rhythm immediately. From the beginning the student plays in four octaves of the keyboard, at first with limited fingers and keys, then with the five-finger span.

Any Primer which begins with quarter notes may be introduced after Lesson 4, although you may prefer to wait until Lesson 6 when the five-finger range is presented.

Starting with Lesson 7, two pages of sight-reading are included in each Lesson. It is through this sight-reading that the student masters the letter names of notes on the grand staff, and gains experience in scanning phrases for hand placement and fingering.

Each Lesson introduces one or more elements, called **Challenge** s, in reading. Students respond well to having a specific challenge! Also, reinforcement is given at the end of a Lesson with **Remember**

Most students can complete **The Magic Reader, Book 1** in eight to twelve weeks. After six weeks, many students are ready for supplementary books such as those by James and Jane Bastien, Katherine Beard, Jon George, Lynn Freeman Olson, Elvina Truman Pearce, and John Robert Poe.

Emphasis on letter names of keys and notes should be delayed until drills are introduced. Best results are obtained if the sections marked **Read** are worked out by the student at home, with only enough help from the teacher to insure that the assignment is understood.

Counting aloud while playing is recommended as an integral part of the reading process, even though students need not count aloud in everything they practice. The skill of being able to count while playing is an indispensable part of good sight-reading.

A parent's attendance is recommended for a young beginner's lessons. Between lessons the parent can direct the child to walk beats and play note values and to assess if the counting and playing are without hesitation. After page 44, the parent can help the child learn letter sequences by drilling "Say three letters up from G; three letters down from B," etc.

When having the child write notes on a chalkboard, give directions as if at the piano. Rather than asking just for a high C (page 12), make the direction to "write a high C for the right hand." When steps are introduced (page 16), use of the chalkboard can help catch any confusion quickly. For instance, the child is apt to write a descending step to the left instead of the right.

The following is the melody for "Ebeneezer Sneezer" (Book 1, page 5).

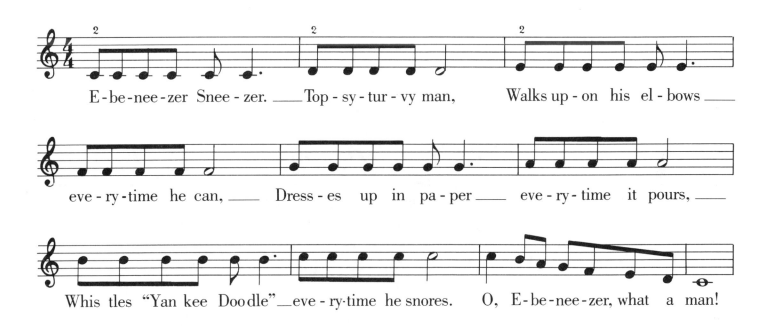

In **The Magic Reader, Book 2** the student will continue to learn the symbols used in notation, plus dotted quarter and eighth notes, and eighth rest followed by eighth note; and to master the names of the notes on the grand staff as well as some ledger line notes. Daily sight-reading is included with each lesson, with more for hands together. Fingering is expanded beyond the five-finger range to include crossings, stretches, and contractions.

Most students can complete **The Magic Reader, Book 2** by the end of the first term, although for some students it may be advisable to delay Lessons 5 and 6 until the beginning of the second year.

The Magic Reader, Book 3, intended for the second year of piano study, continues the lesson format of **The Magic Reader, Books 1** and **2**. It provides a solid foundation for counting upbeats and syncopated eighth and quarter notes. Daily sight-reading is included in each lesson. The feeling for tonality in the major mode is developed through arpeggios and scales in the keys of C, F, and G. Ample reading material is included for familiarity with those key signatures.

About the Author

Louise Guhl's fascination with how students learn led to the development of **The Magic Reader** series. She is an independent piano teacher in Dassel, Minnesota, who is also popular as a clinician. In the past she has taught pedagogy and class piano at the University of Minnesota, the MacPhail School of Music, and Concordia College (St. Paul).

After graduation from St. Olaf College she studied in Berlin, Germany. Mrs. Guhl has also been a piano student of Guy Maier and Bernhard Weiser, and a pedagogy student of Guy Duckworth. She is the author of *Keyboard Proficiency* for college students.

LESSON 1

Playing a Melody on the Piano

Challenge

To start playing the piano!

To Get Ready *To Play*

Watch and listen as your teacher plays and sings this song for you (page 3.)

Ebeneezer Sneezer

Ebeneezer Sneezer, Topsy-turvy man,
Walks upon his elbows every time he can,
Dresses up in paper, every time it pours,
Whistles "Yankee Doodle" every time he snores.
O, Ebeneezer, what a man!

Play this song with your teacher, using your pointer finger of either hand. Start on this key:

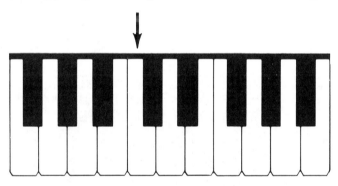

It's name is "Middle C."

Find another C on the piano and play "Ebeneezer Sneezer" starting there.

Find all the C's you can.

Which ones sound like Mother's voice? We call that sound high.

Which ones sound like Dad's voice? We call that sound low.

Play "Ebeneezer Sneezer" in the high
part of the piano with your right hand.

Play "Ebeneezer Sneezer" in the low
part of the piano with your left hand.

You have learned to play a melody! Hurray!

Counting

To learn to count musically.

Walk steadily across the room, counting your steps.

Walk again, counting your steps in fours:

1   2   3   4   1   2   3   4

Walk and count in fours as you clap, or play rhythm sticks, each time you say "one."

You have learned to count beats as you clapped or played whole notes. Hurray!

Whole notes look like this: 𝐨

Choosing Fingers

To choose the correct finger to play whole notes on Middle C.

Number your fingers this way:

Playing Whole Notes

Challenge

To play whole notes on Middle C with the correct finger, as you keep your eyes on the notes.

The note for middle C looks like this: ⊕

Play the notes in the left hand
column with your left hand.

Play the notes in the right hand
column with your right hand.

Never let the counting stop!

You have learned to play the correct finger as you count beats steadily. Hurray!

When the finger numbers are
below the notes, play with
your **left hand.**

When the finger numbers are
above the notes, play with
your **right hand.**

Starting to Read Notes

Challenge

To read notes from left to right across the page using the correct hand and finger.

Play each line of notes from beginning to end without stopping, changing hand and finger on time.

If you have to stop the counting to play the key correctly, practice until you get it right.

Remember

To read notes means to play them.

To practice means to keep trying until you get it right!

Read

1.

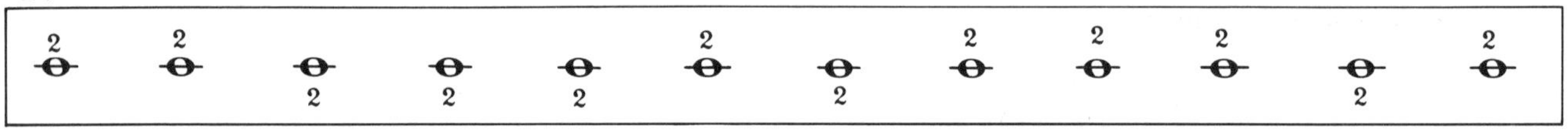

2.

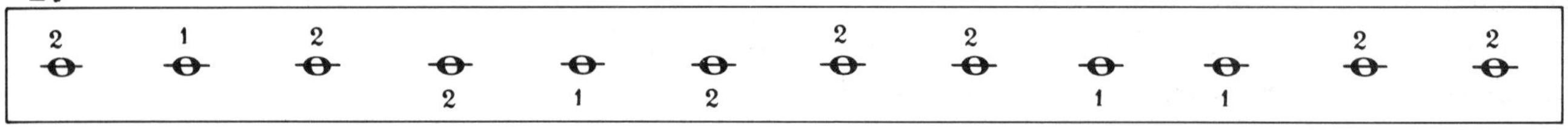

3.

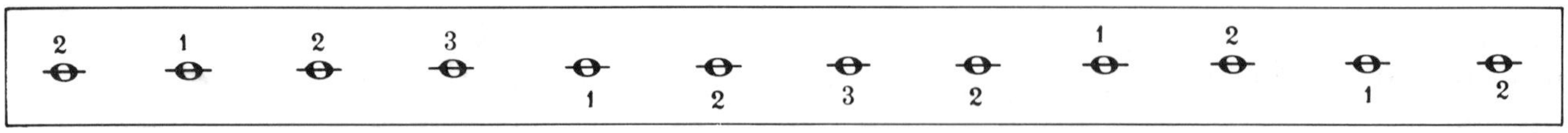

4.

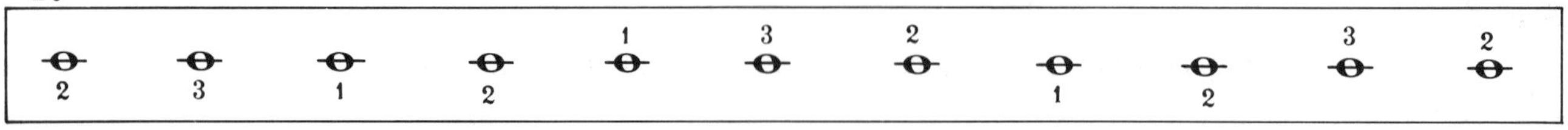

5.

6.

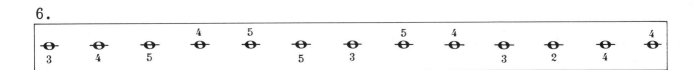

7.

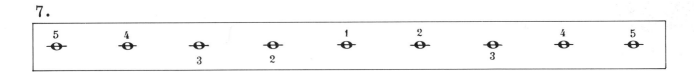

Technique (Technique means skill.)

Drop your hands into your lap.

Lift your forearms up so your hands are level with your elbows.

Let each hand hang loose like a "bunny's paw."

Put your right "bunny's paw" over the keyboard.

Do this exercise while you count four beats:
> On count 1, drop onto a white key with the tip of your third finger. When the key is all the way down, let your wrist drop as low as it feels good.

> On counts 2 and 3, keep the key down as you listen.

> On count 4, bring your wrist up high enough to look like a "bunny's paw" again.

Do that on five different white keys.

Now do the same exercise with your left "bunny's paw."

For Fun

Put the right pedal down with your right foot, and make up pieces about bell sounds: big and little, high and low.

LESSON 2

The Grand Staff

Challenge

To play notes on the upper staff with the right hand, and notes on the lower staff with the left hand, while counting and using correct fingers.

Read

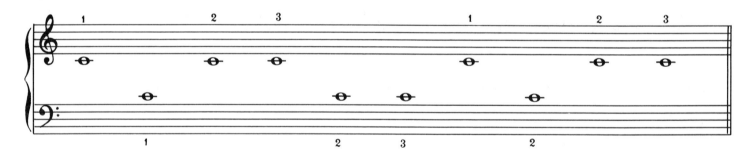

Challenge

To count four beats from one bar line to the next without stopping at the bar line.

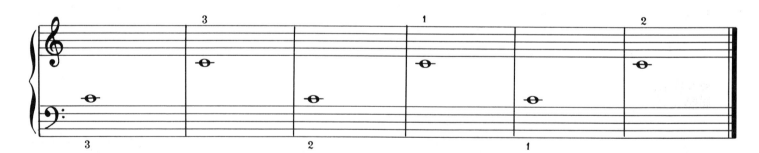

Remember

The space from one bar line to the next is a measure.
You will count four beats in each measure.

Half Notes

Challenge

To play whole and half notes with the correct hand and finger while counting steadily.

To Get Ready *To Count*

Walk, counting in fours as you clap, or play rhythm sticks, each time you say "one" and "three."

You are playing half notes. **Half notes look like this:**

Read

1.

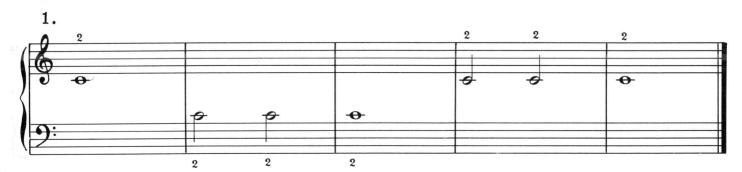

2.

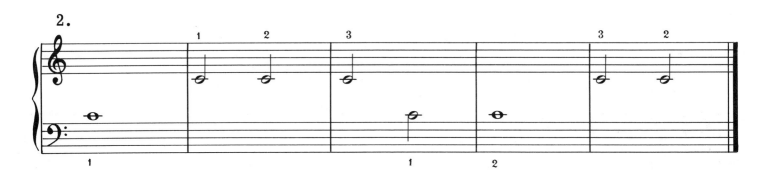

3.

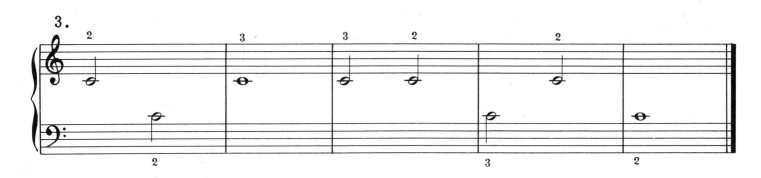

Finding Two New C's to Play

To move both hands to different C's.

Move your right hand from Middle C to the next C to the right.

Skip that C, and find the next C to the right. That C looks like this on the grand staff. It sounds very high.

With your left hand, find the nearest C to the left of Middle C.

Skip that C, and find the nearest one to the left. That looks like this on the grand staff. It sounds very low.

Practice finding the three C's with any finger you choose, but with the correct hand. Play and count without stopping.

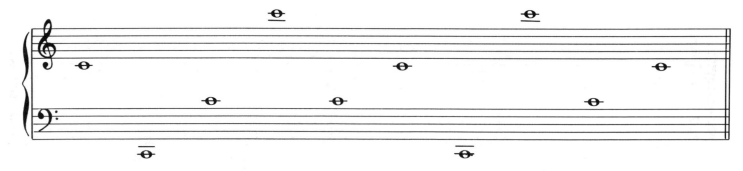

Playing Three C's on the Grand Staff

Challenge

To look ahead while counting.
To move one hand to a different key while the other hand is holding a key.

Read

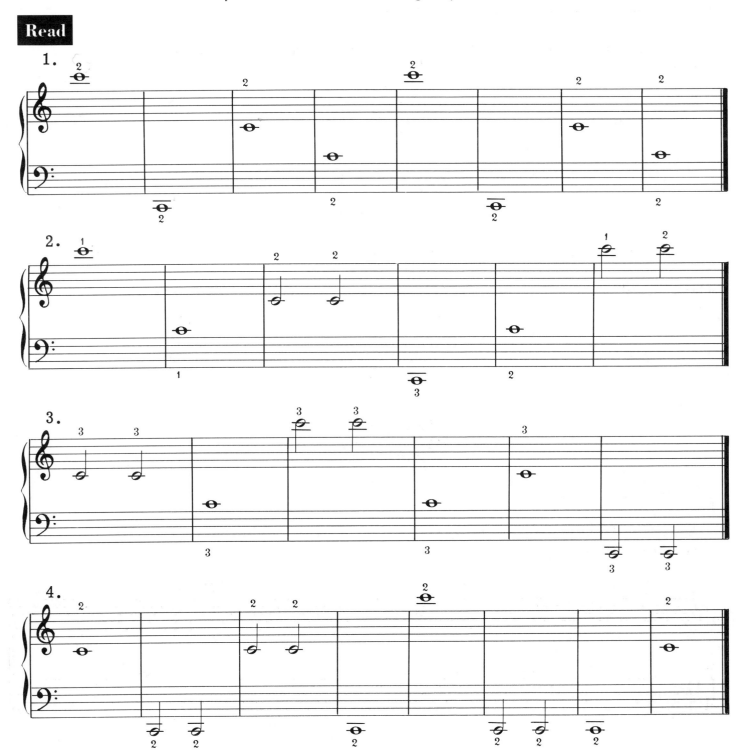

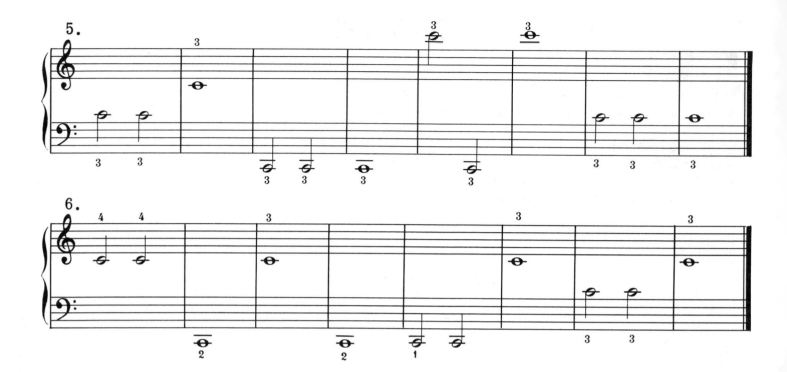

Technique

Play "Ebeneezer Sneezer" with your third finger.

The last time you play each key, make a "bunny's paw" before you move to the next key, and end the piece with a "bunny's paw."

Playing a Melody "By Ear"
(That means playing without reading notes.)

Challenge

To learn to play "Twinkle, Twinkle, Little Star."

Start on any C. Find the melody yourself, or ask your teacher to help you.

Use only your second finger.

Play with each hand.

For Fun

Make bell sounds with black and white keys. Make some bells sound far away, and others nearby.

LESSON 3

Two New C's

Challenge

To play three different C's with each hand while counting without stopping.
To play a repeated note with the same finger when there is no finger number.

To Get Ready

Find the C's between Middle C and the high and low C's you have learned. Play all these C's
several times while looking at the keybord.

Read

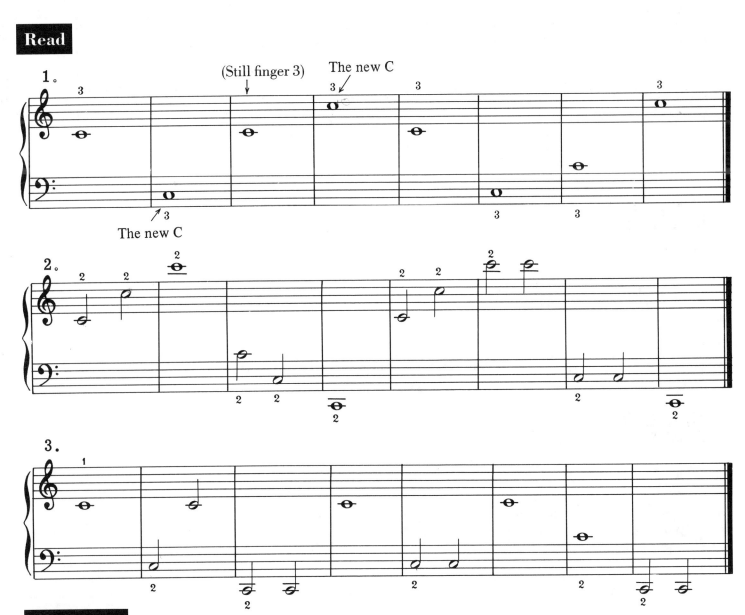

Remember

When a note is repeated, the repeated note is to be played with the same finger as the first note.
There is no finger number printed for the repeated note.

Playing from One Key to the Next Key

Challenge

To play the next finger when you play the next key, without a finger number to help you.

To Get Ready

Play a white key with your thumb: hold it down as you play your second finger on the next key. Feel the spacing, and remember how it feels.

Move your thumb up one key, and with your eyes shut, play the next key with your second finger. Feel the spacing.

Repeat this exercise with the other hand.

Now try it with fingers 2 and 3 in each hand.

Read

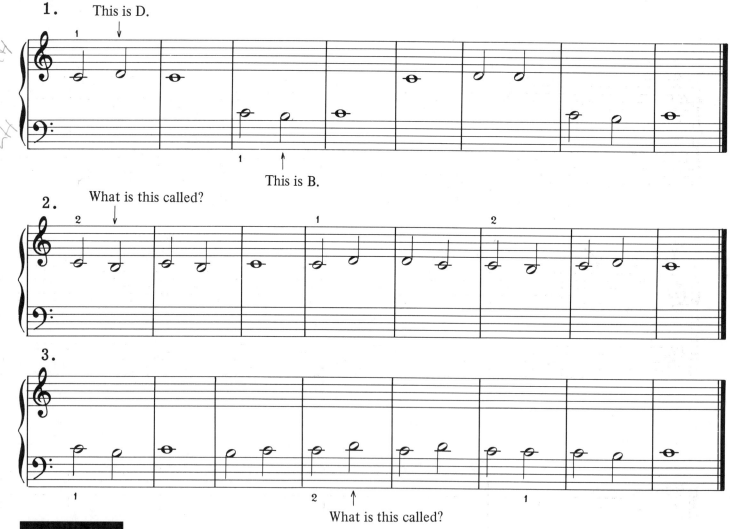

Remember

"Next-door" keys are played with "next-door" fingers and have "next-door" letter names.

Technique

Play these next-door keys with next-door fingers.

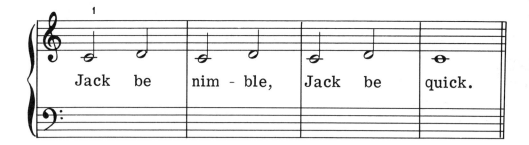

Now play "Jack Be Nimble" starting with your thumb on D, then E, and other notes.

Play again with fingers 2 and 3. Repeat this exercise with the other hand.

Remember

The finger you use to play the first note of a piece will be used for that same note all the way through the piece, unless a finger number tells you to change.

Playing "By Ear"

Challenge

To play "Mary Had a Little Lamb."

Start on E with the third finger of your right hand.

Find the melody yourself or have your teacher help you.

How many keys does it take?

What fingers will you use?

For Fun

Using fingers 1 2 3, make up melodies for these words: "(Your name), time for bed!"

Make up melodies for Mother to sing, then for Dad.

LESSON 4

Quarter Notes
Skipping a Key and Skipping a Finger

Challenge

To play and count quarter notes.   To skip a finger when you skip a key   To play with a connected sound (legato).

To Get Ready

Walk, counting in fours, and play rhythm sticks on each count.

Read

5.

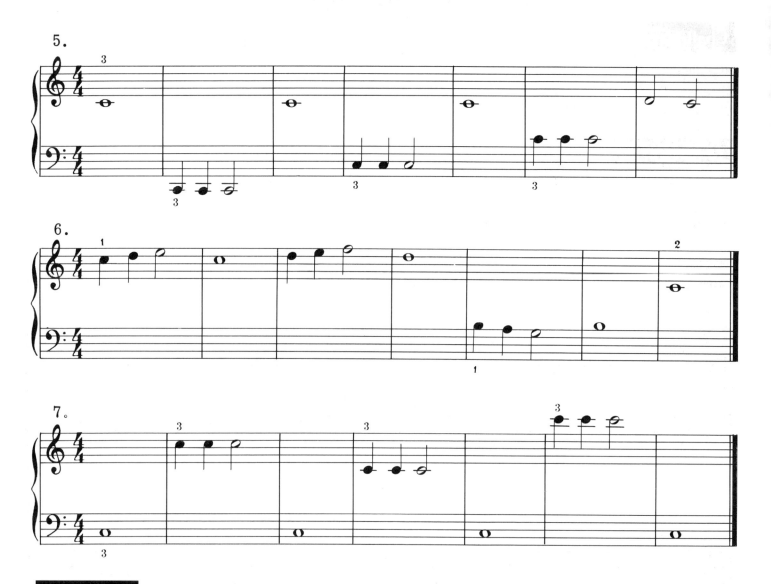

6.

7.

Remember

When you skip a key, you skip a finger.

Technique

Play this exercise using fingers 1 2 3 by starting on six different white keys every day. Play the same fingers in the left hand starting with C B A, then moving to five other positions.

First I | step and | then I | rock.

Dotted Half Notes

Challenge

To count three beats for a dotted half note.
To see the time signature.
To play two hands at one time.

To Get Ready

Walk and count 1 2 3, playing rhythm sticks on count 1.

You are playing dotted half notes. **Half notes look like this:**

Read

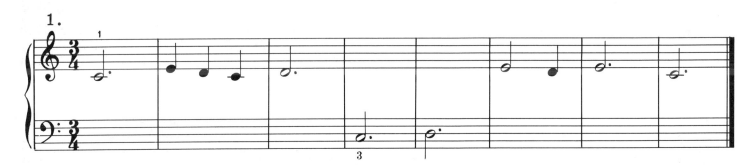

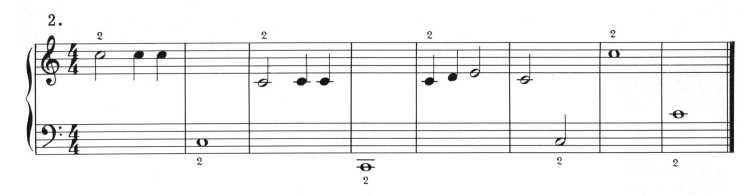

Remember

The top number in the time signature tells you how many beats to count in each measure.

Technique

1. Play this exercise in four different octaves every day. An octave means you move to a different C to play.

I will play pi - an - o ev - 'ry day

2. Play this with your right hand.

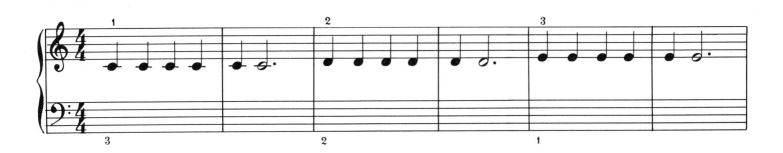

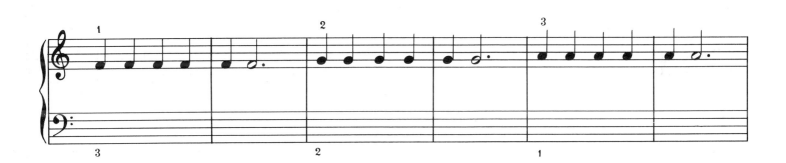

3. Now, play it one octave lower with your left hand, using the finger numbers below the staff.

24

Discovering Sounds When Moving to Different Keys

1. Start "Mary Had a Little Lamb" with your right hand third finger on A. After playing, put an X under the words below that describe how it sounded to you.

Play it again starting on B.

Start on F, then on C, then on G, and then on D.

	Just right	Strange	Really bad
A	_____	_____	_____
B	_____	_____	_____
F	_____	_____	_____
C	_____	_____	_____
G	_____	_____	_____
D	_____	_____	_____

2. Play "Twinkle, Twinkle" with your left hand, starting on E. Then on F, and then on G.

Which one did you like best? _____

For Fun

Make melodies, using fingers 1 2 3 4 to these words: "(Your name), time to get up."

Make some melodies for Dad and some for Mother.

WP190

LESSON 5

Fourths

Challenge

To skip two keys and two fingers when you see a fourth on the staff.

Read

1.

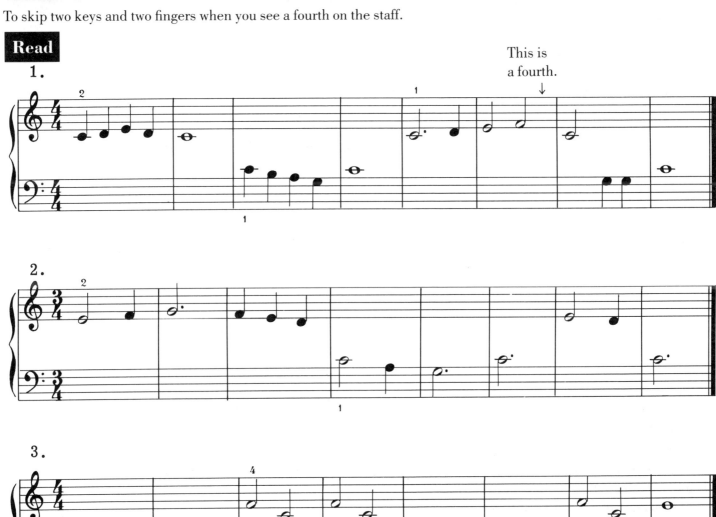

This is
a fourth.

2.

3.

4.

26

5.

6.

7.

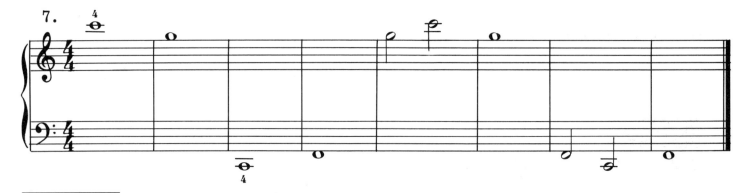

Technique

Play this exercise starting on five different keys each day.

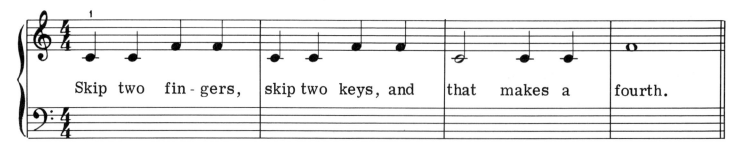

Skip two fin-gers, skip two keys, and that makes a fourth.

Practice the same exercise with the left hand using 1 and 4.

Remember

You skip the same number of fingers as you skip keys to play a fourth.

The Names of the Keys

Challenge

To learn the letter names of the keys so well that you "own" them.

Practice saying the seven letters of the music alphabet from A to A. Then from B to B (B C D E F G A B).

     C to C
     D to D
     E to E
     F to F
     G to G

(Practice tip: it helps to do them several times every day.)

Find all the A's on the piano, playing each one with your second finger.

Then find all the B's.

Practice finding three or four different keys of each letter every day.

Challenge

To play with different kinds of feelings.

Play "Mary Had a Little Lamb," starting on E.
     How do you think Mary feels?

Play it again, starting on C.
     How is Mary feeling now?

Find ways to play that show how Mary is feeling.

For Fun

Play melodies, using all five fingers. Use these words: "(Your name), time to go to school."

Make some melodies for Dad and some for Mother.

LESSON 6

Fifths
Fast and Slow
The Pedal

Challenge

To play two keys a fifth apart with two fingers playing together.
To count fast and slow.
To use the pedal.

To Get Ready

Walk and count two measures in $\frac{4}{4}$ time slowly, then fast.

Walk and count two measures in $\frac{3}{4}$ time, fast, then slowly.

Read

1.

2.

Remember

⌐_____⌐ This sign below the staff means to put the right pedal down. That is called the **damper pedal**. Hold it down to the end of the sign.

When you count slowly, you are playing at a slow **tempo**. When you count fast, you are playing at a fast **tempo**.

3. Slow

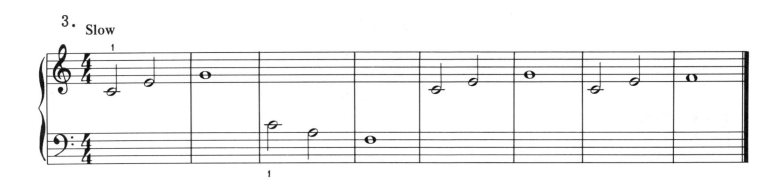

4. Fast

5. Slow

Technique

1.

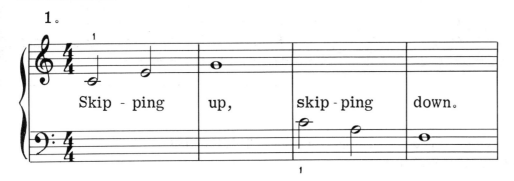

Skip - ping up, skip - ping down.

Continue playing up one key at a time until you have started on six keys.

2.

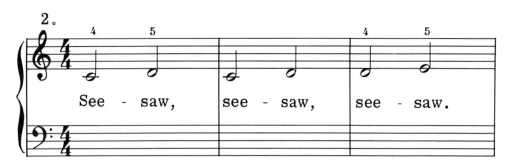

See - saw, see - saw, see - saw.   Keep on going!

Roll sideways from your fourth finger to your fifth and back.

Play, starting on five different keys each day.

Play the left hand the same way, starting with 4 on C, then on B, and continue on other keys.

3.

I will play pi - a - no ev - 'ry - day.

Play on five different keys each day.

Roll your hand sideways towards the fifth finger, then back towards the thumb.

Play the left hand using the same fingers, starting with thumb on C, then on B, et cetera.

Repeat the technique exercise on page 26 using fingers 2 and 5 instead of 1 and 4.

LESSON 7

Whole Rests

Challenge

To listen for silence.

A whole rest tells you to listen for a whole measure of silence. **A whole rest looks like this:**

or this:

To Get Ready *To Count Whole Rests*

Walk, whispering four beats to the measure.

Walk, whispering three beats to the measure.

Walk, counting one measure of silence, then one measure of quarter notes with rhythm sticks in $\frac{4}{4}$ time.

Walk, counting one measure of silence, then one measure of quarter notes with rhythm sticks in $\frac{3}{4}$ time.

Challenge

To look ahead for the next notes while counting rests.

Read

1.

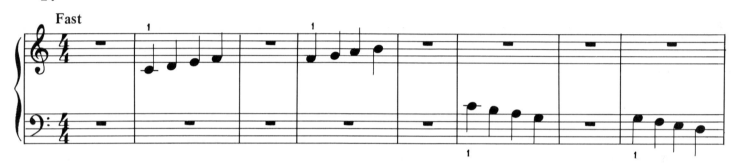

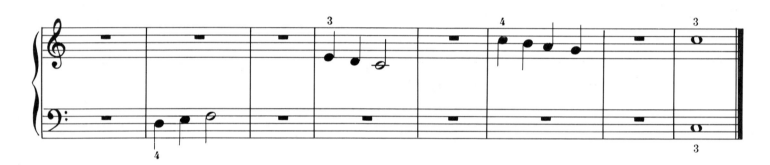

2.

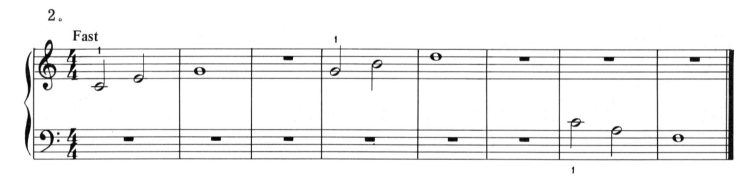

3.

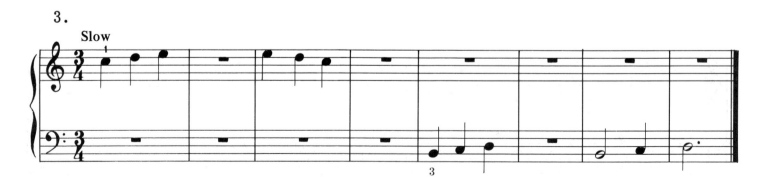

4.

5.

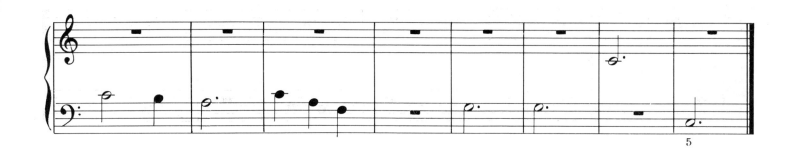

Loud and Soft

Challenge

To push the keys down firmly to make a loud sound.
To push the keys down gently to make a soft sound.

The sign for loud is f.
f stands for "forte," the Italian word meaning loud.

The sign for soft is p.
p stands for "piano," the Italian word meaning soft.

Although these are Italian words, people in many countries know them if they play music.

Technique

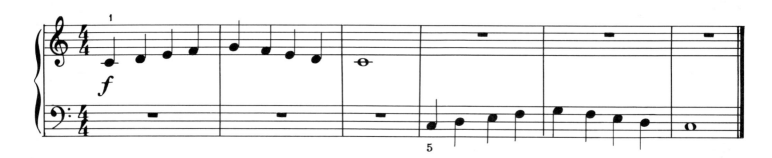

Play the exercise above three times every day, starting on three difference C's.

Remember

F tells you to play loudly until a *p* is marked in the music.
P tells you to play softly until a *f* is marked in the music.

Letter Names of the Notes

Challenge

To learn the letter names of the lines and spaces on the grand staff.

To Get Ready *To Learn These Names*

Point to each line and space and say its name.
The name of the first line in the bass clef is written to help you.

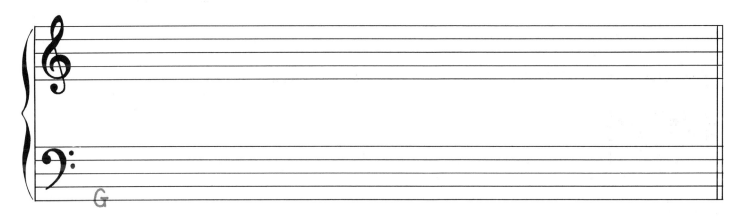

Now write the notes for the five C's you know. There should be *six* notes because one of the C's can be written in both clefs.

You are writing in the bass and treble clefs. Their signs look like this:

Bass clef sign
This is used on the staff
for the ₗₒw part of the
keyboard.

Treble clef sign
This is used on the staff
for the ʰⁱᵍʰ part of the
keyboard.

Practicing Sight-reading

Challenge

To sight-read a new piece every day. (The first time you play a new piece, you are sight-reading.)

The goal is to play the piece without stopping.

Try to get it right the first time!

To Get Ready

Scan the right hand part. (That means look it over from left to right.)

Decide which finger should play the first note, and write that number over the note.

Scan the left hand part and write the finger number under the first note.

Say the letter name of the first note for each hand.

Place your hands on the proper keys, then play the piece just once.

Read the sentences below and put a T after each one you think is true.

1. The counting stopped one or more times. _____

2. I played one hand better than the other. _____

3. I stopped when I changed hands. _____

4. I counted and played without stopping, but played some wrong notes. _____

5. I counted and played without stopping, but missed some notes. _____

6. I did not finger correctly so some of the notes were wrong. _____

7. I played it perfectly the first time. _____

8. I need to play it again more slowly. _____

After you have played it perfectly, fill in the missing word: I had to play it _____ times to get it right.

Play Number 2 (next page) tomorrow, then one piece each day.
Write in the blank (_____) for each piece how many times you had to play it to get it right.

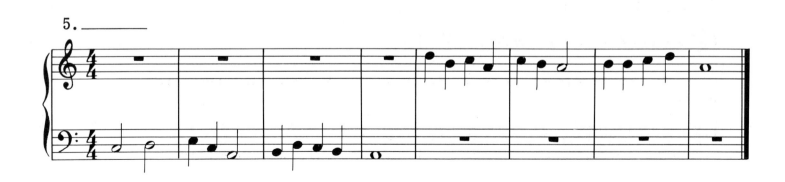

Lesson 8

Half Rests

Challenge

To count two beats for a half rest while you listen for silence.

To Get Ready *To Count Half Rests*

Walk and count four beats to the measure.

Count a half note aloud on beats one and two.
Whisper a half rest on beats three and four.

Whisper a half rest on beats one and two.
Count a half note aloud on beats three and four.

A half rest looks like this:

Read

1.

Ties

Challenge

To hold a key down while you count a tied note.

A tie looks like this:

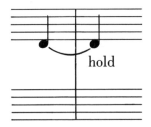

or:

To Get Ready *To Count Tied Notes*

Count and clap your hands for each note to be played.

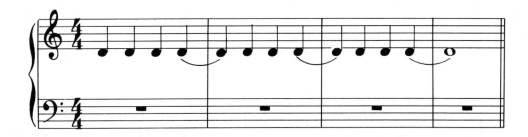

Now play the notes with any finger you wish.

Read

1

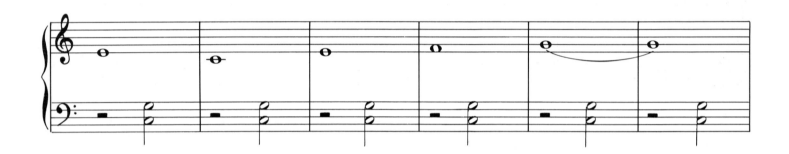

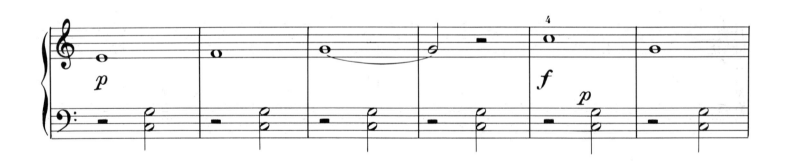

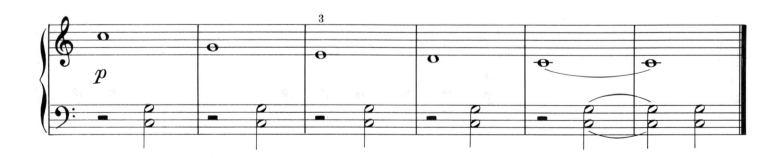

2.

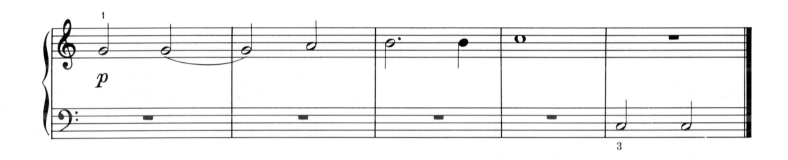

3.

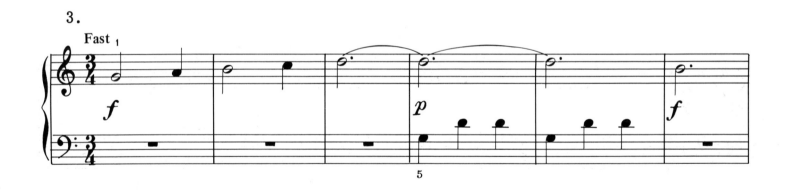

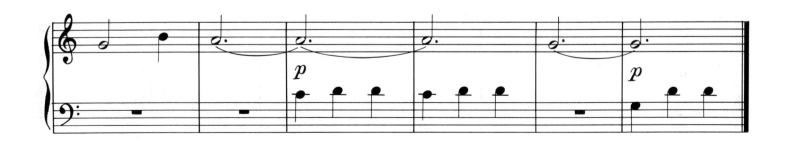

42

4.

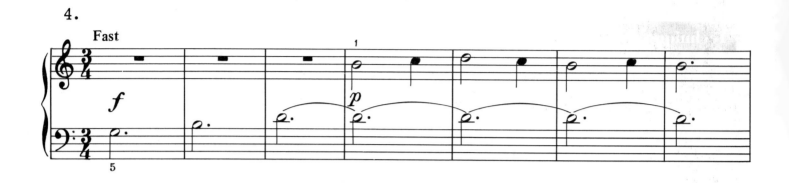

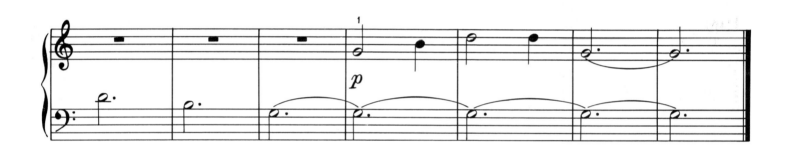

5.

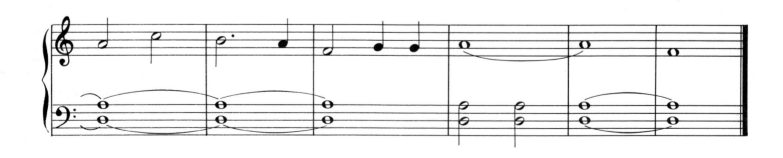

Technique

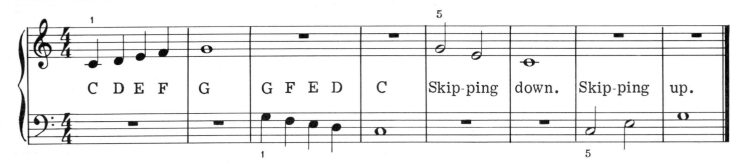

C D E F | G | G F E D | C | Skip-ping | down. | Skip-ping | up.

Look at the keys while you say the letter names of the keys, or the words.

Move your hands up one key, and play the exercise again: right hand playing D E F G A; left hand playing A G F E D.

Play the exercise starting on two or three keys each day until you have reached the C and G an octave higher than you started.

Using Two Hands to Play a Melody and Accompaniment

Play "Mary Had Little Lamb," starting on E, as your teacher plays an accompaniment of fifths with you.

Then you play the accompaniment as your teacher plays the melody. Now play both melody and accompaniment yourself.

For Fun

Play fifths with your left hand as you make up melodies of your own with your right hand.

Play "Mary Had a Little Lamb," starting on A or B and find a good fifth to play in your left hand.

Try "Mary Had a Little Lamb," starting on C, and see if you like fifths with that.

Read

Slow

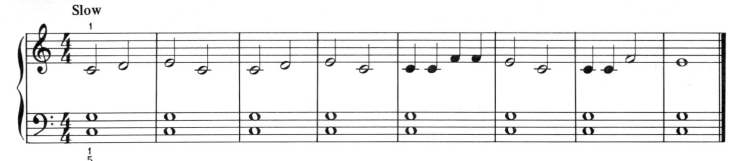

Letter Names of the Notes

Challenge

To learn two G's.

Study the treble staff.

    Find all the G's.

    Name all the notes. (Try to do this every day.)

    Play and name all the notes.

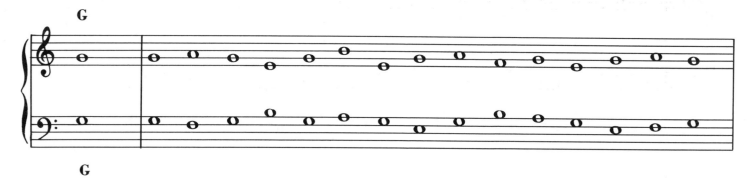

Now study the bass clef the same way.

Daily Sight-reading

Follow the same steps you did for page 36.

3.

4.

5.

Note Review

Set a slow beat and name one note for one beat. Name the treble staff notes, then bass staff notes.

Speed up the beat and do it again.

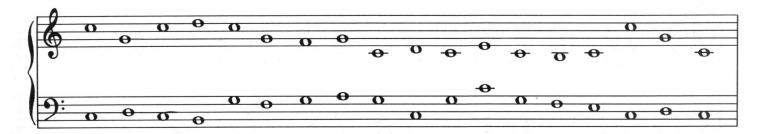

LESSON 9

Quarter Rests

Challenge

To count one beat of silence when you see a quarter rest.

A quarter rest looks like this:

To Get Ready *To Count Quarter Rests*

Walk two measures of $\frac{4}{4}$ time, whispering a quarter rest on the first beat, counting out loud on beats 2 3 and 4.

Walk two measures, whispering the rest on the second beat.

Walk two measures, whispering the rest on the third beat.

Walk two measures, whispering the rest on the fourth beat.

Read

Staccato

Challenge

To play a very short sound, called staccato.

To Get Ready *To Play Staccato*

Practice the exercise on page 49. Play a white key by "scratching" it, curling your finger into the palm of your hand. This makes a staccato sound.

A staccato sign looks like this:

or:

Read

KNOCK, KNOCK!

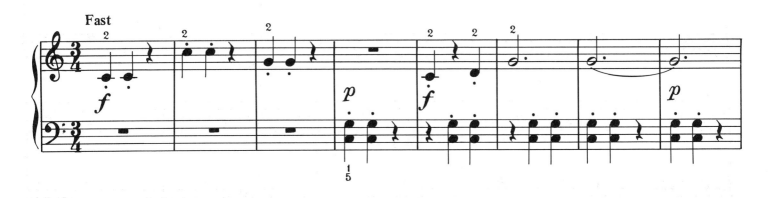

CARILLONS

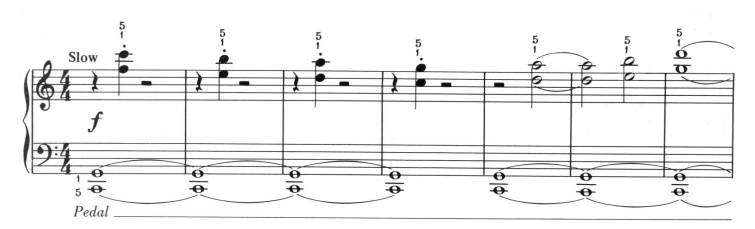

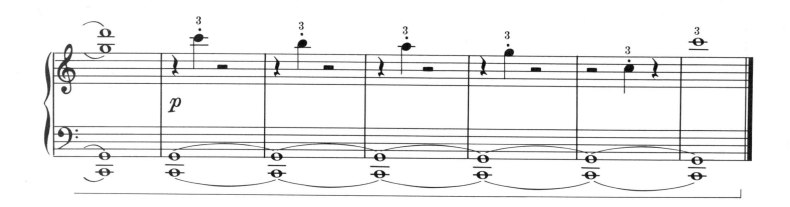

HICCUPS

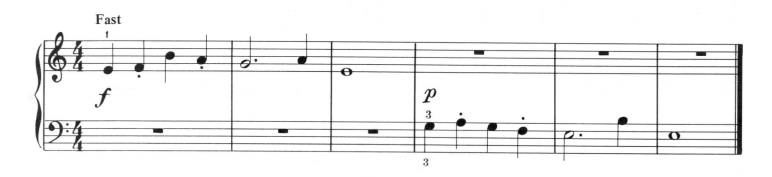

Technique

Bunny's
paw
↓

1.

Play this exercise on each white key until you have played to the next C position.

2.

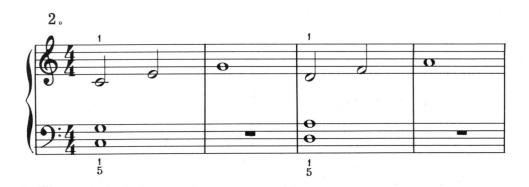

Letter Names of the Notes

To learn treble A and bass D.

Study the bass staff.

Find all the D's.

Name all the notes.

Play and name all the notes.

Now study the treble staff the same way, to find all the A's.

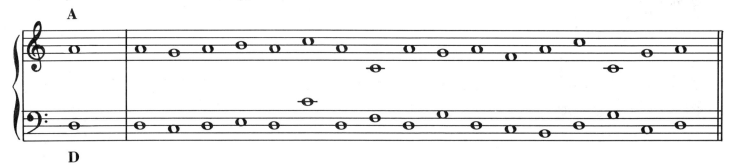

Daily Sight-reading

Note Review

Set a slow beat and name one note for one beat. Name the treble staff notes, then bass staff notes.

Speed up the beat and do it again.

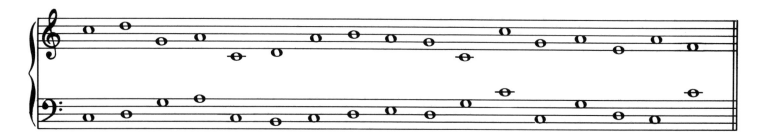